Voices Carry

Mervyn Taylor

Voices Carry

Shearsman Books

First published in the United Kingdom in 2017 by
Shearsman Books
50 Westons Hill Drive
Emersons Green
BRISTOL
BS16 7DF

Shearsman Books Ltd Registered Office
30–31 St. James Place, Mangotsfield, Bristol BS16 9JB
(this address not for correspondence)

www.shearsman.com

ISBN 978-1-84861-497-0

ACKNOWLEDGEMENTS

The poem 'Low' was published in the anthology *Veils, Halos & Shackles*, 2016.
'Death in Mudland', 'Those Who Stayed', and 'The Lesson' appear in the
online journal, *Past Simple*, December, 2016.

Many thanks to Susana Case for her discerning eye and patient ear,
for listening to these voices when at times they tended to grow
garbled or worse, off key.

Contents

for Nancy and Judy

I

Death in Mudland

Poor Professor Perry, what did they
think to find, those thieves running
from your residence, besides books
left over from teaching days in wintry
states, a bottle of preserved plums,

the icebox door ajar. What, climbing
those rickety stairs, did they imagine
the portrait of your wife on the landing
might fetch from a deal in Georgetown,
US or GT dollars exchanged in the dark,

their beady eyes dancing, in the old
wooden quarters of that city. What of
worth did they believe they'd discover
in your suitcase on the unmade bed
in a back room, half-unpacked, mouth

open, dumb witness to their crime,
shirts spread about, and striped ties.
And an army of letters, spilled from
a small valise, intended for friends,
that they'd never receive, only

news of your sad death, of the heat,
and humidity, of the robbers in hurried
scamper, like rodents, one reporter said,
among them three who seemed to be
females, judging by their long tails.

Incoming

We used to clap whenever
we landed, to cheer as the
plane shuddered to a stop.

Now our minds grow busy
mapping the route from
airport to home, the many

places where things could go
wrong, the gifts, the personal
items in the suitcase, stolen.

Coming in from outposts
in Amsterdam, London,
New York, we've grown old

on such flights, undecided
at which end we should
linger, which death

might be better, in snow,
or one where the heat
cooks us quickly, till

we're done, like everything
the sun blazes down on,
the tar, the sand, the sea

making that dueling sound
of satisfaction and regret, of
fires flaring, and going out.

Those Who Stayed

In the small spaces of their yards,
they lodge their complaints:
everywhere there's so much war,
and last night, in the next street,

did you hear that woman scream,
whose boyfriend set her on fire?
How are the children, one asks,
the ringworm, it gone? They'll

exchange pelau for fish, an end
of pork left over from Sunday.
Termites are eating both their
houses, and the boy in America

for some reason, hasn't called.
They'll go back, after a while, one
to her sweeping, the other sitting
by the phone, in case it should ring.

Enough

What if, suddenly, the spate of killings
were to end, the blood run, a tilted
river, out to sea. What if, after one

final eruption, the violence should
slide like lava, and harden. Then,
we could continue tying the children's
laces, patting their heads once

they learn to do it themselves. If
the sky were to become the ceiling
in a dream, the sea a scuffed carpet,

we might begin to forget the sound
of a neighbor being strangled, the thief's
warning to his partner, *Enough!*, the
engine running in the getaway car.

Only Son

for Colors

You showed me the boy, when
he was three, red and skinny, your
spitting image. Years later, when

he was only thirteen, you worried
that he'd done his first job, some
dirty work that left him, the gun

heavy in his pocket, to get back
however he could, from down by
the sea. Now a grandfather,

you describe how the police
found him, out on the highway,
head one way, leg another, how

they wouldn't let you near the
folded wreckage, the bodies of
those who had called him, *Come*

go, spread like the fingers of so
many arms, his face no longer
the spitting image of anything.

Blue Lights
after Jack W.

The man who would be Prime Minister wants,
more than anything, blue lights, and sirens

that squeeze shoppers against store windows,
their faces mirrored among the mannequins.

Here he comes now, hidden behind tinted glass,
official D of A insignias on both front doors—

our Minister of Agriculture, who should never
be in a hurry, when one considers the trees,

how slowly they grow. His wish is to one day
have outriders, with reflective visors, chrome

fenders, grins wiped clean during training.
Get out of the way, you who suspect he's only

going to get a shave and haircut, and then
to see if those ordered seeds have been planted.

Security

Outside Maraj Jewelers,
his face is stern, the bore
of his rifle frightening.

What would happen,
I wonder, if two men
with smaller guns

surprised him, what if
they managed to get
their muzzles pressed

against his parietal lobes
and in wild reaction
he brought his weapon up,

pointed towards
that dining terrace
above Excellent Trading,

where a couple sits, holding
hands across the formica,
searching for something

sparkling, the man's
proposal stopped
in mid-sentence,

the blast tearing into
the midday, the stones
in the store unseated

from their settings,
unfit for engagement
or wedding, suddenly

too small, too blown
into fragments, into sparks,
the shaking hands of the clerk

rearranging the display,
if the guard were ever
to let his guard down.

Alma's Advice

Who are the boys we'll root for,
when they're all dead or gone away?
Where is the cluster of houses
we'll indicate with a wave,
meaning where we grew up, where
we had our first glimpse of secret
flesh, covered with fur.

Where are the girls we ran after,
desire to caress them singing
in our bones, where are those
mothers who came after us, arms
flailing, who knew the kind of fire
in smell, in touch, hidden in hollows
and in botanical gardens.

Who are the strangers now
running wild in our country, darts
for eyes, clubs for fists, hit lists
embedded in text messages.
They make our play seem childish,
our centipedes curl away from their
scorpion sting, all our treasures turned
to chaff in the evil of their conferences.
Who ever heard of shooting a man
while he held his baby in his arms?

Where is Alma the hairdresser who
taught us woman-wiles, a snort of brandy
before she sat us down, who said it's
possible to become these things:
stone, shelf, roof, step, ravine, flooring.
But not while keeping the heart
that makes us human, not without

eating out of some hand the berries
of forgetfulness, as she showed us
her man, sneaking through a hole in the
fence, while the gate stood wide open.

A Kind of Valentine

in memory of Asami Nagakiya

When you come to the place in the world where you think you belong, how do you know? By the local who understands your language? By the freedom you feel?

1.
The hum of traffic goes unbroken
round the Savannah, a couple waiting
forever to cross by All Saints.

The seat near St. Ann's is still
missing half its back, from the time
a car jumped the curb, killing two.

I think of where we would walk
if you came to visit, what you would
say, in the midst of the flowering poui,

about the murdered girl whose body
was found here, the pans playing
holy songs, far from anything arranged

for the Carnival that so went to a man's
head, he tried to hide her
among the yellow blossoms.

2.
I will walk you round this Savannah,
because we've always boasted
of its beauty, because it's where

all our love and all our craziness
take place, where our horses have raced
and our rapists, greased to the belly,

have crawled and come upon careless couples.
I will show you where not to go at night. But
I cannot help during the day, when

it is bright, and a hundred thousand people
offer invites, and behind the masks, men
are not always who they say they are.

Bad Dream

1.

O, troubled island, go back to sleep,
back to your peaceful ways,
when your weeping was quiet,

back to when you were like
the brown dove, and no one
remarked your coming and going,

when your wings were silent,
and life was mostly about nesting.
Go back to being the workman

measuring fifty square miles, with
your ladder, in your khaki, fixing
signs that blew down in the storm.

2.

In the Carnival, you thought you saw
the devil, and hid under your bed.
Now come and see—his mask

is paint, and paper. His horns
are melting in the sun. Go back
to the dream before the dream,

before the mucus stuck your lashes
together, and you thought you had
gone blind. To the time when

everyone had arms held out to catch
you, and the ground was as soft
as breadfruit patterns. Go back

to sleep, take up your dream
at the point before the fire started,
when what fell was dew, not ashes.

Not on Any Map

Fast as I bail, this boat fills up,
the shore no closer
than an hour ago. The Indian
on the beach is still a dot, shells

invisible in his basket. Tell me
where I'm bound for, again?
The waves make me giddy,
and salt has set my skin

to stinging. I had no idea
how separate these islands are;
they scatter in the sunlight,
crabs to their holes.

Was it always like this,
learning the hard lesson,
Carib killing the Arawak,
landfall hard to make, looking

for mountains, three to be
exact, a bed of oil forever
bubbling? Who set me
adrift, I forget that too.

I lost one oar, then
the other. One night I
thought I heard singing,
dreamt of women

with frangipani flowers
in their hair. But now I'm
confused—the whittler
has made of this rock

a pencil, of another
a book open to heaven,
stars dropped to its pages.
And all around flying fish,

squadrons attacking the air
and falling as if wounded
back into the sea,
the currents pushing

this way and that.
I remember an inlet
with a bridge I crossed
long ago. The rails were white,

and red birds flew overhead.
Ibises, I believe.

The Village Where Dreams Are Kept

Charlotteville, you wake up early, full
of cock crows and whispering leaves.
The mist lasts long on your hills,
the harbor quietly rocking your boats.

Your children are first to be heard,
their accents strong, their elbows
when they come into view held out,
to keep strangers from hugging them.

The sweep of houses from the hilltop
to the semicircle of your bay resembles
the dive of blackbirds as they pilfer
from your nets, moonshine their favorite.

Your forest stops abruptly at water's
edge, the sea going from blue to green,
sea grape clinging to mahogany. It is
all part of Gang-Gang Sarah's legacy,

the salt sprinkled as she tried to fly
home to Africa. Now you own yourself,
tourist come, tourist go, capsized
boats in pictures they take, vessels lit

by lanterns swinging from their masts,
leaning, leaving. At this end of the island
you are protected, villagers quick to
assemble, if one dream goes missing.

Tobago Love

In the new harbor, a cruise ship fits snugly,
waiting for Customs to board. After papers
are checked, the tourists will go ashore,

out to the reef, or the Nylon Pool, so clear
they can count their toes, the eco-minded
to the bird sanctuary. There was

a couple, hacked nearly to death
last year, now back in London,
the wife blind in one eye, her husband

limping out mornings to their mailbox to see
if the promised aid has come. Nothing,
except an invite from the island's

House of Assembly, to return, and stay for free.
No one mentions them, not the new guests,
not the waiters, who've been warned.

Belmont, the Beginning

1.
In the foothills of the mountains
that keep hurricanes from coming in,
next door to a Shango yard, I born.

When I was five we moved to
the flatland, down the lane where
Friday nights we still heard the drums,

near where my grandfather ran a livery
service in two yards, coaches in one,
horses in the other, bit and tackle

hung high in the room where drivers
ate, Aunt Ursula among them, fond
of the noise and clatter, till Lottie,

my grandmother, took her by the ear,
washed off the horse smell, led her
to a life of spinsterhood and gardening,

stern table manners while tending
magnificent ferns that would climb
her fences, and flowers that won prizes.

2.
This Belmont was the enclave where
police could never find their quarry,
where Spanish, Indian and Black

would mingle and marry, curly-headed
children filling the lanes of the place
the poet called 'City of Tailors',

Uncles Syke and Milton part of that
trade, one good at jacket, the other
a pants man, one upstairs, one down,

for years not speaking, some quarrel
over wives. Next door was Uncle Tertius,
tall, political, floor walker at Hoadley's,

yellow tape round his neck, still deemed
not good enough for The Belle, but whom
he still managed to marry. At every corner

was a cobbler, and in the alleys
that joined and snaked everywhere
were seamstresses like my sister,

whose wedding dresses flowed down
the Anglican steps. Her stays held bosoms,
her sewing room crowded with women

who leafed through magazines, conversing
on topics of the day. They were charming.
My father came and went, hardly noticing.

3.
We had, too, our myths: Belmont Jackass,
escaped from her owner, dragging her
chains through the midnight quiet,

the restless spirit of a runaway slave.
Then there was the ghost of the rapist-
policeman, in the days when three killings

a year was plenty, found guilty of murder
in the Savannah, whose lost stick betrayed
him, his daughter, when she was shown,

exclaiming, 'Daddy's stick, Daddy's stick!'
The Savannah itself was its own myth,
that green field where love was made

a million times over, against the white
racetrack railing, behind the boxes full of
cricket implements, under the cannonball

tree, and over by the tennis courts,
in garages behind the Princes Building,
the giant samaan hiding us from the world.

4.
And female spirits like the La Diablesse
and Soucouyant flew, and women like
Miss Ruby sucked their teeth and spat

to clear the air of gossip and bad-eye,
while I read books in one of those houses
so close together we could see right

into our neighbors' bedrooms, as they could
see into ours, the buttons on my father's
uniform shining, before he rose in his gruff,

accustomed silence, gulped his blue-rimmed
enamel cup of tea, and left to conduct his train
through a country still asleep, and dreaming.

Macaw

1.
The parrot is calling names.
You don't like the one he's
given you—*Don't Leave Me.*

His mate has left him too.
He spells her name in seed
on the bottom of his cage.

2.
You'll do anything for a night
without dreams, a sleep
without sweat. To feel better,

you sit at the piano with
a vase of fake flowers that
won't wilt while you play.

3.
One of your neighbors,
you're not sure who,
purchased this bird that

hears you turn,
restless. He can
mimic unhappiness

dripping like rain through
branches, a woman dragging
her slippers up the road.

The Goats

Long-ago things return to mind:
the Chinese place behind the bridge
whose owner died with his recipes,
the black and white tiles underfoot

at Bishop Anstey's Seniors' Dance,
the smell of Diane's dark perfume.
Midnight on the Tobago ferry, under
a full moon, a man playing his pan,

a foot holding it steady. My head
rested on the arm of an Asian
girl, wishing in my dream
she'd never move. And then,

there was the day I ran home to tell
my dad, I had passed the exam,
when he could hardly raise himself
from the bed to hand my uncle

the money, saying, go, buy the boy
the bike. I remember the goats,
how they used to drag him, his
necktie hardly holding up his pants.

I am kept from falling by these things
that follow me. They save me, even
in dreams, Sally's kids in a huddle,
chewing their cuds, calling my name.

Forged from the Love...
(opening line of the Trinidad & Tobago National Anthem)

Remember Marjorie Beepatsingh, big-boned
policewoman, famous for arresting men
who didn't stand at attention for the anthem?

In the square today, even the vagrants stand still.
They remember her lifting men
by the back of the pants, carrying them down.

Her spirit must be around here somewhere,
the number of rapes and murders climbing
since the year began.

They are afraid she might arrest them, even
those with no pants. Hold them by the skin,
walk them tippy-toed through the crowd.

Remand Yard, Frederick Street

Outside the high, yellow wall, families wait.
Their conversations break off every time

the small door in the gate opens, and they
catch a glimpse of the yard inside. I remember

when cousin Earl was waiting trial, and a guard
let the door stay open long enough for us to shout

greetings at the prisoners crowded behind a tall
barrier, how Earl, being short, had to jump and yell:

I'll be... alright...don't...worry...I'm...holding...on,
his voice cut off as the gate clanged again,

and we were left outside, milling around, like
these are doing now, jumping every time the bolt

is drawn back, hoping, maybe a truck coming out,
might force the gates open, wider this time, and

there he is, a nephew, crossing the yard in the late
afternoon sun, carrying a bucket, sweeping, anything.

Heart Man

In Barbados, the story's told about a man
on the lookout for anyone walking alone,
whose heart he'd sell to racehorse owners,
to feed their horses, to help them win.

The human heart, they say, especially a man's,
will make a horse run very fast, sometimes
not stopping until it came to the sea, and
sometimes, not even then. The locals

laughed at us when we vacationed there,
as you insisted I walk on the inside wherever
we went, to the beach, to the racetrack,
Lady Godiva, odds 20-1, winning by lengths.

A Carnival Story

The King Sailor and the Dame Lorraine
sway, as pretty in their dance as
in their costumes, while they wait for

the Midnight Robber and the Dragon,
the blue devils that stab the air with
pitchforks, the moko jumbies reaching

up to the sky. And the Bookman,
who will explain all this
to the children. Perhaps Isaac,
retired from mas,

will show the young Black Indian
how to perform, correct his speech
and his weapon, show him
where it's pointed wrong.

Rock the Boat

(a dance in the sailor band at Carnival)

The matadors lift their skirts,
their men holding the ropes.
The purpose of the long, red nose
is to poke fun at the sailor

asleep in the whore's gallery.
They tell Shore Patrol his ship has sailed,
and they pay the musicians, who sing a song

about how the water down Macqueripe
is too cold, how the U-boats
dive under the U.S.S. Woodie,
rocking the boat.

Destinations

1.
Friends complain my passport
is full of the same destination:
Trinidad, Trinidad, Trinidad.

It's time, they say, to go somewhere
else, where there's no Carnival, no calypso
leading the nation through the town

on foot or on stilts, masqueraders
waving, always waving,
neither in welcome, nor goodbye.

Time to go someplace not so crowded
with memories, someplace full of surprises,
with monasteries behind high walls,

statues of poets reading,
galleries where people sit listening,
attentively. Where the officials

in customs study your face
curiously and allow you two weeks
to take it all in.

2.
High in the mountains of Quito
my daughter and her mother
wrapped in colorful blankets

posed for pictures and sent them
as postcards on the back of which
they wrote, See, see? But

even as I read, I see myself
sitting by the Queen's Park
Savannah, watching the nurses

from Port of Spain General passing
inmates let out from St. Ann's,
and schoolchildren, some of whom

still say, politely, Good evening, my
passport in the house in the lane filled
to the last page with Trinidad, Trinidad.

Pop, Fathers, Uncle

These are my new names, given me by complete strangers. Suddenly I'm related to the young man who moves over in the taxi, to the girl clerking in the hardware store who asks, *Uncle, you getting through?* I suppose I am. I've come through crowded Port of Spain, misjudged a high pavement, at the last minute righting myself. I've managed to remember where the taxi stand is, patiently waiting till I hear, *Belmont, Fathers?* I look for the priest who must have been put out from the Cathedral, which is under reconstruction, for a cleric collar. How do all these people think me family, from the tall-hatted Rasta smoking his cheroot, to the Indian who shaved fins from the sliced carite in my bag. In what way do we resemble?

I take the seatbelt the woman in the backseat is shaking to remind me, Buckle up, Daddy. I snap it in and catch a glimpse of her in the rearview mirror. She is at least as old as I am. I'm tempted to say thank you, daughter. But I say thank you, dear. Thank you.

Race Gone

When horses were in the Savannah,
cantering, as in that Walcott poem,
I liked the steam of their early
breath in the paddock, a groom

nose to nose with a skittish one.
I miss them in the clear light,
and I miss the dust as they came
round the bend on races day,

the old cemetery like an ancient
walled city among whose ruins
the dead lay with their camels.
Inside the white rails were tables

with red and yellow squares,
and wooden rings that never fit
over bottles with fat bodies, girls
and boys tossing pennies.

Small men born to ride jostled
for position, jerseys color to color,
mounts neck and neck. But mostly,
I feel their absence when I see

the empty sand track, no Jetsam
or Mentone breaking into a run, no
frilly dresses, no stopwatch clicking,
measuring a horse's chances, or mine.

Voices Carry I

1.
Not always clear, mostly they
are soft, whispered across water,
the sound of oars dipping and
rising, dripping all around them.

What they have to say is not
always pleasant, is often keening,
a flute played too close to the ear.
The sea is the back-up singer, and

darkness the conductor, baton
raised over the hills, the voices
of the mad making children spin,
till they fall down, giddy.

2.
Long ago they sang in fedoras,
a tie with a palm tree, a silver belt,
pleats the width of two fingers,
confident, boldfaced kaisonians.

The musicians crossed their legs
and tuned up saxes with bent keys,
the piano with the stained ivory,
the shoes with two tones tapping—

one two, one two, stories from
the mouth of the bards, old
with complaint, young with vigor,
of love's lament, and scheming.

And in the dangerous front row,
where one chances ridicule for being

so close, *picong* and spit flying,
critics sit and take in everything,

waiting to see any tic in the details,
if they miss the fact that it was a
Friday, not Sunday, that it was Sel
who played for the dance, not Joey.

3.
The hecklers do their work. Tourists
have to work it out for themselves,
the noise the cane made grinding,
the noise of the whip amid the stalks,

the sound of rain and blood together
in the flood, washing away houses,
the island itself shrinking until all
stood crowded atop the highest

mountain, singing into the waves,
heard in faraway cities, ignored
in heartlands where the ocean's
only a dream. The young among us

sing faster and faster, pots
coming to a boil, their hearts racing
from the video, from the gunfire,
from the absent relatives, their feet

covered with the sands of beaches,
the clay of other parishes, Kingston,
Kingstown, Georgetown, Bridgetown,
Port of Spain, Port au Prince, the boat

piled high till it can't hold any more,
the song climbing the air since there
is no more mountain, only clouds,
like octaves, and after them, only sky.

Voices Carry II

Between the hills and the sea,
when the night is dark and faces
hard to make out, voices carry.

Between midnight and morning
in the narrow lanes, while children
sleep, big people talk, their voices

carrying between Belmont's
close houses, drifting eastward
on currents, as far as Matelot.

They speak of plans to build
and demolish, they argue cost,
before they grudgingly agree.

Voices carry a note to the judge
in the privacy of his chambers.
Partitioned by wooden blinds,

they drop to a register so low,
he must ask them to repeat
what they thought they heard.

Voices carry news of the return
of a long-gone son, his approach
silent, like a skiff over the shallows.

Voices speculate over reasons
for his return. Full of welcome and
warning, voices carry him home.

II

Nostrand Avenue

1.
Nostrand runs all the way from one
end of Brooklyn to the other, where
going with a girl into the Windjammer,
my friend met his wife coming out.

Round midnight the King's County
crew gets off at Clarkson, speaking
of being so tired, of early retirement
and which handsome doctor they'd

like to take home, once the house
in Toco's finished, and the old bones
hold up. They know every scar, every
bullet that goes off in East New York.

Nobody knows why the young man
who got on at Eastern Parkway cried
and cried until he got off at Empire.
Mother dead, father dead, who dead?

2.
Now where Nostrand intersects with
Fulton, down from where the crowd
crossed between Terrace and Fightback
on Saturday nights, the hipsters sit,

eating roti and drinking lattes. Upstairs
on Franklin, Evelyn's mural has faded,
the bald proprietor gone, his parts
scattered all over the island. Preacher

closed his barbershop, where once
you could get anything, from suits

to shoes, and went back to Marabella,
moving into the old house his mother

left him, declaring war on the squatters.
He hardly recognized Suzy, who vanished
the night they danced in Frontrunners,
and he ran out on the avenue, looking.

Ode to the Painted Bunting

(which appeared suddenly, last fall, in Prospect Park)

O beautiful bird, what were you
doing so far North? Good thing
the weather had remained warm
well into December. They had you

surrounded, those photographers
with their zooms; their tripods must
have frightened you, an army of
legs in the bushes where you tried

to hide. The woman I had invited
for lunch said she'd never seen
anything like it—your blue head,
green wings, the red of your body,

the way everyone was down
on hands and knees, wondering
where you'd come from, how long
you might stay. I was unimpressed

until I saw your picture in the paper.
It made me think of my friend Fox,
who told me how exotic birds are
brought in, in toilet rolls, wings

pinned to their sides so they would
not whistle, who once lost forty of
them in a fire, but none as lovely as
you, the wind ruffling your feathers.

The Birthday Boy

My brother's in his nineties now,
and I'm thinking, should I continue
our hundred-dollar exchange this
year, me sending him one in late
August, he in December sending it
back, broken into twenties? Why

bother, I'm saying, I could just
get a bottle of rum and head out
to Queens, although lately he has
to hide to take a drink, since that
bout with gout, his wife keeping
an eye on him, her pacemaker

forcing him to go easy. What about
a hat, I consider, though he hardly
goes anywhere now, and doesn't
fuss much about how he looks. In
the picture on my dresser people
who come over think he's a movie

star, black Paul Newman, I kid you
not. It was taken back when he was
an upcoming light-heavyweight.
His girlfriend Lucille was a beauty
with a whispery voice you had to
come close to hear and doing so,

you'd catch a whiff of that perfume.
Come to think of it, what could I get
for him that's better than what he's
had already. I confess I followed them
one night, just to see where you'd
take a lady like that, lucky guy.

The Lesson
for Doc Long

A Brooklyn man walks down a street in Lagos
with his Nigerian friend, worried one of his buddies
from the States might see them holding hands.

He keeps finding ways to let go, pointing in surprise
at every little thing. This makes his friend wonder,
Has he never seen a cow before? A woman
with a basket on her head?

Suddenly, the African shouts, "Look, a tiger!"
"Where?" asks the frightened man, grabbing his arm.
"Nowhere. But if one comes, it's okay to hold my hand."

Lemongrass

Nature can't decide this evening, snow or rain.
We watch it come down, and order everything
on the menu, my grandson identifying the vehicle
splashing by outside, as not just truck, but flatbed.

He chews the duck, flies his plane off the tarmac of
the table, Gates 45 and 92, Grandma badgering him
with questions. I sit at the far end, happy for the family.
How could I ever have rejected this! For some imagined
adventures, cardboard creatures, folding in the rain?

We taste each other's food—the curry, the ginger,
the coconut, the green ice cream.
My son's wife's belly almost touches the table,
a second child. I'm here, I'm gone away, swimming back
for everything I left behind, adding a line

to the toast they ask me to make.
Salud, my dear family, forgive me for coming in and out
of your vines, but look how beautiful you are, twined and
running along each other's bones, new growth urging you on.

Learning
after Da Chen

On the Greyhound bus returning from a visit
with my daughter and new grandchild,
I read about the life of a young Chinese boy
who wants to go to college, to major in English.

It is very difficult for him, learning to sound
the letters, especially the 'e'. It is hard for him
to understand why people say 'Good morning,'
before knowing how it is going to be.

There are other obstacles in his way. There's
no encouragement from his community.
Such is life in his little village. They believe
those ambitions belong to imperialist cultures.

He knows that the hardship of farming is
not for him. The sting of the sun, the calluses.
He has also flirted with the violence of street
life, and knows that, too, is not for him.

So with his friend who smokes too much,
he finds a spot in a field, in the middle
of the wheat grass, and spreads his books,
the lunch his mother prepared, and begins

to make up for lost ground. Suddenly, as I am
reading this, the bus makes an unexpected turn,
and the driver announces he has to pick up
a passenger who has been left stranded.

We search, and finding no one, get back
on the road. I return to the story: the boy's in
his classroom, taking a test. But my mind is on
the man somewhere along the highway, waiting.

Our Fathers

My brother and I had different fathers. Mine died
when I was thirteen, his he spotted when he went
to work one day, on the roof of an adjoining building.

I've tried to answer his grief with a story of my own,
of how one candle seemed to heat the entire house
while my father stopped breathing in the next room.

Between us, we keep the memory of our mother alive,
his of a woman scrubbing floors, mine of her passing
a hand along shelves, singing Some Enchanted Evening.

My brother lives in what was a cul de sac, that is now a
thoroughfare. The room where my father died was the
size of the elevator in the one where his dad succumbed.

Where Do They Go
for Elva and Nola

When we say those near death
are traveling, what does it mean?
When they say they want to go,
where do they want to be taken?

Home to a gallery in Tunapuna
listening to the grandchildren
of the neighbors who are so glad
for the things from America, or

home to Linden Boulevard, cars
flying like crazy on the way
to Kennedy. Or home to heaven,
a place like Santa Cruz where

they say even snow is possible.
What do they mean when they
say they're ready, begin rolling
from side to side? Why do they

start cussing late in life, they who
never used profanity before,
who were so gentle and giving
they took in other people's children

and made us sleep on the floor.
Where do they go once they cross
ninety, and wear that smile,
as though they can see

someone who went before,
pointing and showing the way,
when they say, *Goodbye,*
when you miss me, I gone.

Crazy Ursula
for Brens, in memory

I remember your excitement when you first
described the kurta you'd found at the bazaar,
for fifteen dollars, imagine, fifteen! Such a lover
of bargains you were. And I joked, where would

you put it, with the rest of the things that left
no room for your husband in your bed, with
your sandals that made a carpet on the floor,
so when you swung your feet over to walk,

you had to clear a space? The one that was so
sheer, standing before the light you looked
like crazy Ursula by the standpipe, naked, after
the man stole her money and ran Venezuela.

Away

The red-haired girl
who works at the Lois Fuller restaurant
has disappeared. Her car's in her
driveway, but she's nowhere around.
It's been three days.

That was the story back home.
We looked out across the bow of our boat
headed for Pinel Island,
the sea and the boat an identical
bright blue.

I took a picture, which would prove
nothing: water, wood, and
orange cushions on a beach of strangers.
Show it to them anyway, I said,
her hair braided into jets of flame.

Bones

He follows his mistress' every move,
pretending to chase chickens.

He shifts when she shifts, finds
a high wall from where he can watch
the ice in her glass melting.

He cocks his ear when she reminisces
about the dog she owned before, Whitey,
who also shadowed her everywhere,

her husband one day finding him
stretched out under the house of a man
with whom she was having an affair.

It's a story she loves to tell,
shoes off, wiggling her toes,
keeping Bones from falling asleep.

Low

for Sara Kruzan, who killed her pimp

Did he shoot you up,
put you in a low room,
make it difficult for you
to stand, did he push

you out on cold nights,
say come back with gold
or not at all, did he walk
and watch your limbs

move in the dark,
did he set you up in
low-lit places, bang
on walls till they shook

your eyes, your teeth,
your insides, did he
promise you nothing
more than x's to mark

where last you stood
dripping, smoldering,
the fire going out, until
what was left drifted

into a latitude where
his loaded gun became
yours, a rescue vessel
making the sound

of kittens being drowned,
the gurgle of his voice
going under, the song
your soul was singing.

The Dye Job
for S. C.

You write, it's only thirty degrees
where you are in Africa, so chilly
you'd snuggle up with an impala.

This morning, grey roots coming in,
you had to choose between a white
salon and a black, finally deciding
upon the cheaper of the two. Today's

Botswana Gazette tells of a careless
woman killed by a lion. But your guide
smiles and says you are safe, as long
as you don't panic and run. I think

if you met a lion, it would just stare,
puzzled by your red hair. Together
you'd both go after an impala, awed
by each other, one hungry, one cold.

Not Cricket

My poet friend has grown careless.
He's in love; metaphors abound.
Now when he writes of revolution
and struggle, the lines waver, revert

to descriptions of her curves, kisses
thrown in her direction falling
back to earth, like bombs falling
on a field outside Jaffna, where

he learned the game of cricket,
the danger of a ball that almost
took out an eye. When she grows
angry enough to break his glasses,

he pretends they're playing, runs up,
delivers, imagines he's throwing
rockets, helping the rebels behind
the borders of the northern provinces.

Sometimes, after they've made love,
as he listens to her breathing,
he wonders if they'll ever move
the barriers, if his words will ever reach

the encampments where the Tigers
are hemmed in, while his eyes
sweep the darkened room,
his poems somewhere under the bed.

Terraces of Haiti   (A Trinidad Poet Visits)

1.
Here the fortified homes of the privileged rise,
the girl on guard duty hardly able
to pull back the heavy iron gate,
though the truncheon she held said
she would do her job, no matter what.

Shadows lay deep in the valley below. Word was,
people were burning cars and tires in the red zone.
Calls were coming in from our host's guests,
that they would not be coming,
that the roads were too dangerous to drive.

But through his high windows, music was playing.
An updraft of pepper from the kitchen
made the eyes tear as we climbed the stone steps,
our drivers headed for the security post,
their creole soft, conspiratorial.

2.
In our company was a man from the radio station
who'd lived in exile in Miami, and a dark woman, her man
a head shorter than she. The young editors of *Haiti Now*
constantly pecked at their phones, and reported
bursts of fire along a highway, while the video man
tinkered with wires that ran around the room.

I recited something about Ayiti, the earthquake's rumble
felt everywhere. I borrowed the creole word *lamayot*
from a story by Danticat about Carnival,
the lady with the short man smiling when I said
what the *lamayot* had in his box, that people paid to see.

I thought of the vendors rising next day before six, when
business transacts almost as furiously as it does at twelve,
of the dry river beds we crossed on the way to Les Cayes,
of roads choked with people selling everything, from
bicycle pumps to laces, about the changes in government
announced differently, depending which radio you listened to—

Radio Ibo, Radio Melodie, or the one blaring in our vehicle,
the driver in halting English saying he *liked* the government,
how his village had changed for the better, putting his fingers
like a closed flower to his lips and making a kissing sound… *mwe!*
The problem with Haiti, he said, is Haitians don't like Haitians.

And I thought about the bootblacks whose shoeshine kit
the SUV from the American Embassy ran over,
how in plaintive patois the boys complained, while
the armored vehicle leaned, two tires on the pavement,
as if it had all the time, all right to be there.

Port au Prince

City of ground that shudders
beneath boys on motorbikes

whom women trust
to take them up hills

where roads disappear
between houses

Ground that waits
for them to sleep fast

for the boys
to bring them down again

early in the morning
their small heaps of oranges

growing in this city
of no more room

A Trinidadian Recalls
Celebrating His Birthday in Pakistan

In Islamabad, black-suited lawyers are being beat up by
Pakistani police. My friend Tony's wife is anxious to know what
will become of the project she started for abused women there.

She wants to go home, but he's afraid to accompany her.
The last time they fought over her relatives,
throwing sucked bones under the table.

Then there was that warlord from the Khyber Pass, still angry
that my friend had let the women at his birthday party
remain in the same room as the men. In Trinidad, Tony said,

we all dance together! They had first met in Washington,
he and his wife, at a funeral for which the paid mourners
did not show up, too busy wailing for their own.

In Dreams, All Things

In dreams I translate a whole
slew of languages into my own,
so in any city I find I can speak
with the outdoor diners at a café

about the quaintness of houses
surrounding their harbor,
about the parts of their history
so horrible, they'd rather forget.

From Bruges to Lisbon, they'd
rather I don't mention the skins
flayed from bodies, the totems
of missing heads, the libraries

minus the pages that tell the story
of how many hands were cut off,
while they sip their morning coffee
and I stop, like Longfellow's wedding

guest, to interrupt a conversation—
who's getting married, whose aunt
has the tumor—to relate treacheries
tucked into dead vaginas where

no one would dream of looking.
No one even looks up in wonder
at my fluency, how a black man
in Tudor outfit gained access

to these garrets and these shores.
Where is my boat, they wonder.
But not for long, since I might touch
on another subject, dregs of which,

like the grains in those mugs, might be
too bitter, my dream becoming real,
as, uninvited, I take a seat, the waiter
staring as I order, no milk, no sugar.

On the Run

1.
They have no flag, the
name of their country is
printed across their faces.

They learn as they travel,
what will buoy them up,
what will sink the minute

they let go. By land, by sea,
by land again, they count
to see who's missing,

who threw himself overboard,
his last words rising as bubbles.
Who can translate, can anyone?

2.
They are not running from their
conscience, from some demon-
bird whose eggs they've stolen.

They believe in prayer, they
are not guilty of ignoring God's
warnings, Allah's commands.

3.
On the run, these are
the thoughts they exchange:
you are fleeing / I am running

from what / I don't know
who came to our house / did
they come to your house, too?

Do you know, mister, do
you, woman, do you, old man,
why we are throwing our children

across our shoulders, leaving
grandmother behind, do you
believe the clouds will be merciful?

They are afraid they may forget
their own names, words that
did not survive the crossing.

In a Handbasket

The world's moving fast, and the poet
who waits at the crossroads now finds
he is in the shadow of the earth as it
begins to explode, country by country,

his poems scattered among the papers
of other citizens—certificates, warrants,
wills—files they consider important
more than his verses. So those left alive

are free to examine the business of the
dead, a signed confession, an affidavit
a judge refused to try the case without,
a lien on someone's property.

What will the poet write about now:
the way a building falls, how a man fires
point-blank into another's eye, never
blinking, the moon's crazy dispatches?

It is old news the river brings, if it flows
at all, red as tracer fire, reflecting giant
cedars, from the days when, unclogged,
it leapt through mountain gorges, when

clouds dawdled in womanish poses,
applied rouge to one cheek, then the
other. That was before the wreckage
of planes tumbled down to sleep

at the bottom of the sea, passengers
still strapped in, staring straight ahead,
black box pinging in the dark, music
for the fish, until bored they swim

away. On land, those who remain sane
shop listlessly, carts creaking through
the aisles of unperishables, by evening
walking down the rows of seats

in theaters where tragedy follows farce,
actors forgetting their lines, the prompter
not working. In the departure lounge
at every airport, security goes through

bags, and finding nothing but books,
seizes these, too. There is a place where
all comes to a standstill, but the world
is not there yet, is still letting lovers sit

in the new house telling their dreams
until they realize no one is listening,
not the cat wandering out of doors, not
the daughter from a previous union. And

the shortcut the poet once took to arrive
early is sealed off, the news broadcast
in a style he never would have chosen—
offhand, minus metaphor, minus life.

III

Friend of the Poet

Dear Fernanda, how's your house
in the vale, and your Volkswagen,
is the window still broken, the rain blowing in?

How's the poet, does he still take
his typewriter to the beach? Strange—how
the poem persists, however crazy the poet might go.

I recall once, driving through St. Ann's,
he picked up a young lady, handing her
several pages he'd been working on.

I think of her now, poor girl, asking to be dropped off
long before we got where she was going.
And I wonder how you, an Italian,

manage to survive the tropics and someone
who has so edited his last letter,
I can barely make out the words.

Widow's Peak II

I thought my father would
live forever, the widow's peak
guarding his forehead.

The night he lay dying
in the next room,
I dreamed of walking
into the ocean.

And when my feet could
no longer touch the bottom,
I heard his words of caution:
Sea have no back door.

The Dream Thief

The black horse means you will travel,
the naked man is a thief who stalks you nightly,
the leg hanging from a hammock represents a task
you are yet to finish, and yes, you should worry,
the sea is encroaching on your land.

You should sleep facing the window.
Even the dead dream. They knock
the ashes from their urns, and foretell heavens
and hells; they cross their bones and give
each other five.

This is a land where people
still wrap their money in cloth. They go digging
when I arrive, thinking me the robber from last night's
confusion, the head in a burlap sack, the fire
like the one in Mittelholzer's room,
growing hotter by the minute.

The Dead Bird

for Suchitha

You found it on the floor near your bed and cried,
as if you had something to do with its dying.

It must have come in through the patio doors,
I said, and couldn't find its way out of your room.

Maybe it could see outside through the chink
between the blind and the windowsill, watching

friends and family dart through the open air.
It's none of your doing, or bad luck, or anything.

Sometimes something separates us, like now,
that for all my explaining, you won't understand.

Cascadura

Old Fish, you remind me
of how slow you are to die,
how you continue to jump
in our kitchen sink, eyes

staring out of ridged scales,
ancient enough to have
your own myth, the scent
of your flesh an iodine

that finds me wherever I am,
so I still see your folded body,
strung on a knotted vine.

Lake Whatsitsname

Cosby told a joke once about diving, somewhere upstate,
in late spring, into a lake that looked warm. With trembling
voice, he called to his wife, "Come on in, the water's fine."

I still smile, picturing her face, wondering if it was true, or
if he'd made up the whole trip, the sun glinting off the lake's
surface, the water colludingly calm, inviting. I see her

shake her head, back away, toward the car, hugging
her shoulders as if to say, "That's alright, no, thank you."
One early June, at Jones Beach, you encouraged me

in the same way, to jump in, though there was a definite
chill in the air, and only one other, a he-man in speedos,
splashed around. You shivered as you beckoned come,

come. I look at Bill these days, his face drawn, his trials
taking their toll. It's hard to laugh, thinking of how very
convincing he was, how warm he made the water seem.

Three from the Garment District—

1. Charlie

Charlie, head packer twenty years at Talk of the Town Coat Co.,
watched the boss yell the day it was snowing hard and the short
Cuban guy came back from lunch blind drunk, singing *Nunca,*
like the beginning of a sad Spanish song, when the shipping
supervisor said to keep his coat on, these coats needed to go out.

When he sang *Nunca,* again, they told the Cuban he could pick up
his check on Friday. "I will pick up my check now," he growled,
a meanness in those eyes making the secretary scurry to the office
and make it out quickly for Mr. Becker to sign, who then shouted
for Charlie to get *his* coat on. And when Charlie said he couldn't go,
he had a cold, Mr. Becker screamed "I'll knock you down!",
shaking a fist under Charlie's nose.

"Then I'll lay on the floor till the union man come," said Charlie,
his face behind his thick glasses sweating. Over the cutting table,
the long blade stayed in the same position it was when all this
started, all eyes going from the Cuban offering a swig from his gin
to the black man, who, looking down at his shoes, walked back
into his cubby, pictures of his two beautiful girls smiling in the dark.

2. Dapper

Dan was the company salesman, *and* spy, judging by
the skinny he brought back about other showrooms.
A sharp guy, salt and pepper, peaked lapels, the old

Jewish ladies would touch his tie, wonder if they
might get the spring coat for less than factory price.
He never remained on the floor, just long enough

to pick up samples, then on the road again, Bronx,
Queens, Secaucus. The only time he stayed
more than an hour was the day two burly men

cornered him, their noses grazing his face, before Murray,
sixty-two-year-old shipping supervisor called out one
of their names—Marty, saying he remembered him

from the old days, that he wasn't scared of him then,
and he wasn't scared of him now. That's when they
backed off, and Dan went through the front doors,

for the first time not flirting with the receptionist,
not stopping till he got to street level, where he stood,
looking up at the seventh floor windows, sweating.

3. By the Piece

This is how they count the number
of garments rolling off the factory floor,
coming out the dark like some magic
several hands have worked, the seam,
the ream transformed into skirts.

And often amid the clatter a noncitizen
longing to go home might kill off a family
member, fake a funeral she must attend,
sneak away, a drama no one pays
much attention to, long as the pieces

add up, as long as I stand in the middle
and keep charging. Let's ship the shit out—
the boss is allowed to call it that. It's his
place, his machine cutting along chalk lines,
his racks trundling through the streets.

And she'll come back, nobody knows how,
raise the rope along the border and slide
under, no longer Maria, but Francesca,
a light relit when the sun caught her far
from these premises, without her worker's

label. She'll take up where she left off,
confide that the hand that stroked her hair
was still alive, and flinch at the supervisor's
bark as he reminds her it's only a half-hour
lunch, that she was six pieces short, all told.

Points Beyond

My dream puts me at the water's
edge, where the train runs out of
track, commuters getting into
parked cars and driving away

before I can ask, what stop
is this, what arm of Long Island?
The deranged man, did he walk
through the 4.45 already,

is this before, or after his siege?
Drenched after such dreaming,
I smell of salt and marsh land.
I'd plead guilty to any charge

at this hour, as a man unsure
of where he'd been all night,
no one to swear she was right
here beside me, not knowing

when I may have crept from
the bed, gone to what seemed
the end of the world, in the half-
light, something silvery gleaming.

Burying Kings
for Pete

Folks lined the streets to see that British king, his body discovered
beneath a parking lot, dug up for a royal parade and second burial.

In the no-man's land between
East New York and Bushwick,
we laid Pete out in military grey,
black cross on left breast pocket,

a style between Viet Nam
veteran and Rastafarian. We
watched the flag folded and
handed to his wife, who said,

we're not taking any chances,
we're burning our boy right away,
sending him back where he came
from. Then his son intoned, half

American, half Trinidadian:
Kings belong in royal tombs, or
at least under a breadfruit tree,
their ashes shaded from the sun.

Samson's Plea

O moon that goes from full to sliver,
and all shapes in-between, I forget
which one is perfect for wishing,
which not good for cutting hair.

I looked through the back door
last night, the frill of the curtain
sweeping my face, and you swung
like a basket just above the hill.

This, I thought, is the one that
will spill everything, if I'm not
careful, the secret of whom I
just made love to, the regret

I feel seeping in. There's
a cloud that hides your handle,
that sends your porous light
radiating across the heavens.

If you won't take back what
I cried for when you were full,
at least let my locks grow long,
let me bring their temples down.

Love of the Sea

after Tiphanie Yanique

On purpose, the fishermen burst their
eardrums, so they can stay under longer.

They live on one of those atolls past the reef,
on its shores a mountain of shells, rising.

They go back to their homes singing,
the note of a great anemone held long,
calypso karaoke at the bar.

Their boats are named Rosie, Herminia,
after girls jealous of the sea's whisper,
the smell of seaweed in their men's beds.

Things I Can't Throw Away

Like the garlanded Buddha,
a gift from a fortune-telling mom
who came to class on parents' night.

The key my daughter made
with my initials her first stay
at sleepaway camp.

The red shoes with elastic across
the instep that pained like the dickens
after a few hours' wearing.

A diseased plant that refuses to die,
or get well. It sits in a quarantined
corner of the kitchen.

Cards from a mysterious 'Fifi',
signed with puckered lips, whose
husband has since passed away.

A *Jet* centerfold, featuring
an old girlfriend on board a yacht,
somewhere in the Bahamas. And

a simultaneous painting, ripped
across a cloudy moon, done by
four stoned artists around a table.

Twice a year, I declare these things
dead, junk, clutter. I line them up
by the door. Then they beg, and I

put them back, the house squaring
itself and sighing, my new loves
finding space among the old.

Vangi Goes Home

She's going back for more stories, for news
about the boys sent up the mountain, who

did not return from initiation. She's going to look
for a friend seen pushing a cart like a homeless man.

We will miss her, but she must go back to the place
where they make that *click* sound in the throat,

where women walk cocked, stingers in the air,
in case old enemies should attack. Vangi is going

home, in case they need her, and those potions
she secreted on her body while traveling far away.

Hiding in the Men's Room
after Walcott's Remembrances

When finally the lady says 'yes'
to being his mistress, to running away
with him, to being an accomplice
in his next play, to hell

with wife and family, he's terrified
that the pursuit that was safe
as long as her answer was 'no', had
reversed, that the object of his desire

had turned, and was headed
his way, shedding items of clothing,
saying here I am, take me home,
wherever that is.

And so he ends up hiding in
the men's room, as he now advises
his son the artist never to do, but
to pack his easel, his brushes, and go.

Waking Early

1.
Like Grandmother, I start having
breakfast at five, before the birds
wake up in Prospect Park, the subway

motormen stashing their lunch pails
next to the steering column,
tunnels for the moment

free of sparks, voices of
the homeless and bottle herders
carrying in the distance.

I cut short the kettle's
whistle, lay the rashers like boards
beside a house I'm building.

2.
Grandmother, who asks that the blades
of her fan, the glass pendants
of her chandelier be dusted,

as if from below she could see
the accumulation of years, whose
underpants are an embarrassment

when her daughter helps her disrobe
for the doctor, the new ones arranged
in drawers in case of… well, you know.

3.
I begin by saying prayers,
though I haven't for years,
thinking, at this early hour,

how still she must lie,
how her eyes must go like mine
through press and bureau,

looking over belongings until
the light comes in, saying here,
this must be what you're looking for.

Another Part of the World

1.
If my house were higher I could
see the Savannah, green stern rising
and falling on the wave of evening.

I would see the Colonial Seven,
turrets crumbling above the traffic's
wheeling round and breaking off

towards St. Ann's, Maraval and
Belmont, where the hills start,
the lanes narrowing until it seems

you might have to get out, and walk.
I would miss the kites, in homemade
profusion, cloth tails snaking their

knotted lengths over the sky, broken
razor blades wriggling to cut someone
who would chase the paper shape

past the paddock, where horses
used to stamp before being led out
for the race, or the other way, past

the cannonball tree, disturbing
a daytime couple wanting privacy
in an open sepulcher of a place.

2.
The marks of sunset remain
indelible on a washed sky,
purple lines of a child's crayon.

Across from the monument
that mourns the loss of soldiers,
none local, nor the angel

at the top, the samaan spreads
and spreads till there's no room,
a reminder of species brought

from elsewhere, to thrive, to settle
here, in troughs of winds that force
the branches out, out, wider,

till we all can fit in its shade.
On Frederick St., the tennis courts
are gone, but I recall the short skirt

of an old girlfriend, oiled legs
in and out the shadow of the net,
my other flame asking, as we sat

in the theater where my aunt tore
tickets, how come I didn't want her
to play, but carried the other's racquet.

3.
I remember Brigitte Bardot leaning
bare-bottomed against a desk,
showing the lawyer how she'd pay,

before they cut that part, the day
after the movie opened. She was,
for a while, my private pleasure, my

French whore, kinder than the ones
who sat gap-legged in gateways
I only glanced into, whose

legs met in darker shadow. Behind
them, there were half-doors, and
behind those, the blinds some joiner

had crafted, with fleur de lis along
the top and the bottom, soft curtains
stretched in-between. My friend

Harry said one lady chased him after
he climaxed too quickly, and he
tried to kiss her. No romance. Next!

4.
The town, a river mostly dry
cutting it from neck to navel, lies
like a wounded man now. Once

it spelled magic with its mysteries:
Maple Leaf Club on Charlotte St.,
a steel band rehearsing classics

in the secret garret, notes played
with fingernails, musical bombs
to be dropped on Carnival day.

On shopping days, barbers wore suits
under their aprons to meet seamstresses
and hairdressers who came to town.

And when the girls peeped over their
swinging doors, they discarded those
aprons to display sharp ties and

stickpins, pleats and two-toned shoes
as shiny as tools lined up under their
mirrors. And talk flowed from one

chair to the next, one topic to another,
and the mood changed, depending
upon how much change passed,

or was promised with a wink, while
cards fluttered in the games in the
clubs, and downstairs the barrack yards

hummed with sweet curses, everyone's
business conducted in the open,
anywhere there was room.

5.
And at the heart of it all, the market,
that bustling place, where one could
trust meat, onion, anything to afford

that satisfied hiss of pots on Sunday,
the smell of God's fowl, the leg saved
for the man, provider for three homes,

if he could afford, whatever bought
for one, bought for all. This place,
from wharf to hill a smuggle, from

rumshop to church, exposed, like the
bundle of clothes carried carefully
to the gates of white people in St. Ann's,

or hidden, like coppers stuffed in a bra.
Loud in the evening, like macaws keeping
their customary racket, or crying quietly,

like the boy walking with his broken kite
to find the old Indian who bought him
the thread, to tell him how well it flew.

Glossary of Terms:

cascadura : specie of river fish native to Trinidad, famous for its taste and prehistoric look.

Diablesse/Soucouyant : female spirits.

Gang-Gang Sarah : slave woman of Tobago, who, according to legend, tried to fly back to Africa.

lamayot : Haitian character who charges a price for patrons to see what's in his box.

matadors : name given to women famously known for hard living.

Edgar Mittelholzer : Guyanese author who died by self-immolation.

Mudland : Guyana, so called for its many waterways.

patterns : blossoms of the breadfruit tree.

pelau : local one-pot dish of rice and peas, usually with some choice of meat.

picong : mild insults, demeaning jokes.

Pinel Island : resort island off the coast of St. Martin.

samaan : giant shade tree.

9 781848 614970